Minority Faculty at Community Colleges

by
Ned B. Lovell,
Mary L. Alexander,
and
Laura A. Kirkpatrick

ISBN 0-87367-690-4

Bloomington, Indiana

This fastback is sponsored by the
University of Illinois Chapter of
Phi Delta Kappa International,
which made a generous contribution
toward publication costs.

Table of Contents

Introduction

Community colleges are crucial to American economic progress. They provide access to higher education for millions who cannot afford the traditional university. They serve the nontraditional learner who must have educational opportunities provided at convenient times, and they deliver local workforce training.

The recent emphasis on workforce education has led to increased state and federal support to help these institutions provide expanded training opportunities. With the implementation of the Workforce Investment Act of 1998, community colleges have "become the number one provider of education and training for people who want to enter the workforce, reenter the workforce, or advance their careers" (Bramucci 1999, p. 42).

Minorities are a third of the nation's workforce, and this percentage is increasing. In 1995 approximately 50% of the children under age five living in this country were nonwhite, and a large percentage of these children lived in homes that spoke a language other than English (Diversity Continuous Quality Improvement Team 1994).

More than 5.2 million students took college credit classes at community colleges during the 1994-95 academic year (Phillippe 1997). Roughly 44% of all undergraduates in the United States are enrolled in community colleges. The American Association of Community Colleges (AACC) (1998) indicates that more than 450,000 associate of arts degrees and nearly 200,000 certificates are awarded annually by the nation's two-year colleges.

Two aspects that add to the popularity of the community college are its responsiveness to local community needs and the low cost of tuition. Tuition, on average, is approximately half the cost of tuition at public four-year institutions. The cost of a community college education is further reduced because most are commuter schools, allowing students to reside at home.

For the past 20 years, there has been a consistent increase in minority student enrollment at community colleges. Blacks, Hispanics, and American Indians have disproportionately chosen community colleges as their point of entry into higher education. In fact, minority enrollment increased 61.3% from 1986-1996 (Wilds and Wilson 1998). The nation's community colleges enroll 45% of the black students and 55% of the Hispanic and American Indian students in higher education today (Evelyn 2000). Retention of these students through program completion is an increasingly important challenge.

But the leadership of community colleges does not reflect the student body. A large and growing percentage of the students who attend community colleges are minorities, but the majority of the faculty and administrators are white. Furthermore, few formal steps have been taken to make the goal of a diverse faculty and staff a reality. Community colleges need to implement pro-active policies and programs that will nurture, educate, and place minorities in both faculty and administrative positions to truly benefit all community college students.

The Importance of Diversity

As the nation becomes more ethnically diverse, community colleges will play a pivotal role in educating citizens. However, one of the most serious problems facing many of the nation's community colleges is the shortage of minority faculty and administrators. Though the number of minority students on community college campuses is increasing at a rapid pace, community colleges are not achieving similar levels of diversity among their administrators (Foote 1996).

George Vaughan (1996) found that 89% of the nation's community college presidents were white, 4.5% were African American, 3% were Hispanic, 1.8% were Native Americans, and 1.7% were other minorities. Clearly, leadership at the presidential level does not reflect the diversity that one might expect to exist in an institution committed to embracing equal opportunity.

Also, 87% of the nation's community college trustees are Caucasian and 75% are over the age of 50 (AACC 1998). There will come a time when the profile of the nation's trustees will change. As the percentage of minority trustees increases, there will be more pressure and receptivity for the employment of minority administrators. But this change will not occur unless the problem is addressed.

The issue of faculty diversity is no less important than administrative diversity. Nearly 90% of the nation's community college faculty are Caucasian (Gillett-Karam 1999). The percentage of minorities employed as community college full-time faculty were distributed in the following fashion: American Indian 1%, Asian 3.3%, Hispanic 4.3%, and African American 6.4% (Kline 2000). This is a double-edged problem. Without minority teachers, how can one expect to increase the percentage of minority administrators?

Benefits for Students

The community college is the first postsecondary education experience for many minority students. If they are to be successful, they will need more faculty members with whom they can identify. Most authorities, including the American Association of Community Colleges, recommend that community colleges undertake serious efforts to hire more minority faculty. Indeed, community colleges will not reach their full potential as a catalyst for educational and social progress without increasing their commitment to minority leadership (Bowen and Muller 1996).

The significant presence of minority full-time faculty also can help two-year colleges become more successful in recruiting and retaining minority students. Minority students need positive role models who can help instill higher aspirations for education and career success. Increasing the percentage of minority faculty will provide more role models for minority students and enlarge the pool of candidates for future administrative vacancies. These minority faculty members also help both other faculty members and students rethink their prejudicial thoughts and feelings about the capabilities of minorities, thus improving the organizational climate of their institutions.

The large minority enrollment in community colleges gives them a great opportunity to increase the number of minority students who pursue professional careers. Small classes, low cost, convenient locations, and a learning climate that encourages students to try several areas until they find their preferred career make the community college a logical choice for many students, especially minorities. This is increasingly true when minority students have access to faculty mentors of their race. Mentoring relationships blossom when the participants feel comfortable with each other. This kind of rapport is needed for effective mentoring.

Role models and mentors play a crucial part in professional development, and many students select faculty members as role models. Good mentors and role models can help students reach their fullest potential. Community college students need mentors and role models who can demonstrate successful strategies to overcome barriers and achieve success. Mentors are most effective when they share common experiences and characteristics with the students they are assisting. But few professionals are available as role models for minority students on predominantly white campuses.

Unfortunately, the commitment level necessary to attract minorities into community college administrative and faculty positions is often not evident. Few professionals take the opportunity to debate the conflict surrounding institutional racism and its effect on minority recruitment. The challenge is compounded by competition for trained personnel from K-12 schools and from career opportunities in science, engineering, and technology. These important sectors not only are growing rapidly but also are recognizing the need to recruit minority talent. Left to chance, it will be difficult for community colleges to increase minority employment, especially for colleges located in rural areas.

Three major factors indicate the importance of having minority teachers present on campuses: 1) they serve as natural role models for minority students, 2) they are better able to meet the learning needs of minority students, and 3) they are often bilingual (especially in a predominantly Hispanic area), which helps students transcend language barriers. It is "essential to create a profession that is representative of society as a whole to avoid having a teaching force composed primarily of people from majority backgrounds teaching students from predominately minority groups" (Piercynski, Matranga, and Peltier 1997, p. 205).

Taking a more comprehensive view, Alger (1997) has identified the following four values of diversity.

1. Racial diversity enhances interaction among people of different races on and off campus.

2. Racial diversity improves communications and understanding among individuals of different races.
3. Prejudices can be overcome when people discover how much they have in common with people of other races.
4. People of different races may discover that their political beliefs or interests can provide a common ground for fostering understanding and interaction.

Benefits for Organizational Climate

It is increasingly apparent that more minority administrators and faculty are essential to a multicultural campus. In 1997 the Board of Directors of the AACC adopted an inclusion statement, which encourages all community colleges to increase the minority presence on their campuses. According to the statement, community colleges should be responsible for shaping an environment that mirrors the general culture and creates opportunities for all within the college community to interact with understanding, tolerance, and respect for others. In this way, diversity in education not only serves as a model for the world at large, but it also helps perpetuate social harmony for the future.

Kee (1999), in conjunction with the AACC, conducted a survey of community colleges to find out about the state of race and ethnic relations and the status of diversity programs. Kee found a relationship between campus climate and the presence of minority faculty.

Institutions where minority faculty members constitute less than 20% of the professoriate reported less harmonious campuses. Institutions with more than 60% minority faculty reported more harmonious climates. The AACC recognizes that a diverse faculty is essential to a pluralistic campus.

Education institutions often are slow to change, and sometimes their embrace of tradition causes them to resist reform. In this case, resistance is counter-productive. The pervasiveness of diversity makes it essential for community colleges to embrace diversity. Maricopa Community College District has recognized the importance of diversity and publicly stated its intention to make diversity a major goal of its governing board: "To do otherwise is to continue to insulate ourselves from the very society we are charged with serving" (Diversity Continuous Quality Improvement Team 1994).

Minorities have poor program completion rates and only a small percentage transfer to and graduate from senior colleges. A New Jersey study reported that while 60% of white students graduate from college within six years, less than 40% of black and Hispanic students graduate. New Jersey administrators speculate that the lower graduation rate is due to student financial difficulty, social isolation, attendance, and graduation from public schools with limited resources and minimal academic standards (Fields 2000). Fields notes that there is little hope of increasing the percentage of minority community college faculty and administrators without increasing the number of minority college graduates. A factor that contributes to underrepresentation of minorities in administrative and faculty positions is the low number of African Americans entering higher education at all levels. African Americans continue to receive less than 5% of the master's degrees awarded nationally, and in 1991 African Americans received only 3.8% of all doctoral degrees, down from a high of 4.2% in 1976 (Crase 1994).

Colleges with diversified faculty have more academic programs that successfully recruit minorities. These colleges have found that African Americans are less attracted to education and teaching as a profession due to the lack of desirable role models in those particular fields (Crase 1994). Thus the lack of minority role models in faculty and administrative positions creates a cycle in which the diminished minority presence works against the ability and desire to increase diversity and build a multicultural environment. There must be changes in the way educators recruit, nurture, and instruct minorities. Furthermore, strategies must be developed to encourage high school and college students to consider community college careers.

Barriers to Minority Recruitment

A national study by Opp and Smith (1994) found an increasing number of minority students attending community colleges and an inadequate representation of minorities among full-time faculty members and administrators. All minority groups were significantly underrepresented when compared to their percentage in the general population. Opp and Smith found that 5% of all full-time faculty were African American, 1.7% were Mexican American, 0.3% were Puerto Rican American, and less than 1% were American Indian. For an institution known as "the people's college," this is a regrettable situation.

Opp and Smith identify both attitudinal and structural barriers that hinder recruitment, employment, and retention of minority faculty. The key structural barriers to minority recruitment are economic concerns and the unavailability of minority job applicants in the arts, sciences, and technical and occupational fields and disciplines. The greatest attitudinal barriers are department heads who avoid the issue of hiring minority faculty members by arguing that there are few available minorities in their fields and the assumption by the leadership that minorities prefer jobs in business and industry. Opp and Smith conclude that the structural barriers far outweigh the attitudinal barriers. These barriers must be addressed before there can be an increase in the percentage of full-time minority faculty and administrators.

A study by the National Center for Public Policy in Higher Education concluded "that differences in state policies play a larger role than race and income in determining whether minorities, particularly those from lower income level backgrounds, have access to higher education" (Hurd 2000, p. 18).

William Gray, CEO of the United Negro College Fund, best describes the need to alleviate the barriers to minority recruitment of faculty and administrators that exist today: "Women and ethnic groups now considered minorities are emerging as the new American. The fact of the matter is, that's [society's] future. We can embrace [the] future or circle the wagons and resist [the] future" (Frengel 1999, p. 20). Gray and others believe that the lack of minority faculty and administrators is due to poor leadership.

The Opp and Smith study and a developing initiative called the MidSouth Partnership for Rural Community Colleges (MPRCC) were the impetus behind a five-state study on employment of minorities at community colleges. The recruitment of minorities has become a major concern of MPRCC, a partnership coordinated by Alcorn State and Mississippi State Universities to provide education programs and to conduct research to meet the needs of rural community colleges in a five-state area (Alabama, Arkansas, Louisiana, Mississippi, and Tennessee).

The five-state study looked at both structural and attitudinal barriers. Community college presidents who responded to the survey identified economics and affirmative action as the two greatest structural barriers to hiring minorities. Close to 50% of the respondents agreed or strongly agreed that economic constraints made it difficult to hire additional minorities. Both the five-state study and the Opp and Smith study found a similar percentage (more than 30%) who indicated that affirmative action requirements significantly raise the cost of searches. Although it does cost money to establish and implement special recruitment programs, this should not be seen as a barrier; instead, it should be seen as a routine and necessary investment for institutions if they are truly committed to diversity.

The attitudinal barriers cited more frequently by respondents to the study are:

1. Academic departments avoid the issue of hiring minorities by arguing that there are few minorities available in their field (42% of respondents).
2. A belief that women and minorities are competing with each other for the same faculty and key administrator positions (56%).
3. The assumption that minorities prefer employment in business and industry to employment in a community college (35%).
4. The belief that minority faculty and administrators would have difficulty fitting into the social environment of their communities and that their rural location was a barrier to minority recruitment (15%).

Some colleges do little to advertise vacant positions beyond their immediate areas and among their circles of friends. Thus the claims that minorities are not available, that they will not move to rural areas, or that they are all taken by business and industry may simply mask the fact that these community colleges are not interested in developing a diverse faculty. Caucasian community college leaders and department heads, with tacit approval from their boards of trustees, often allow these barriers to prevent them from recruiting minority members. The "good-old-boy network" and "who you know" still strongly influence hiring decisions when the applicant pool is limited.

President J.D. Tschechtelin of Baltimore City Community College (1999) has concluded that one of the central barriers to minority recruitment in leadership positions is that members of the majority take for granted the privilege of being in power. Thus many people in the majority disdain racial preferences and maintain that success should be based strictly on merit alone. Tschechtelin cites recent federal court decisions, which have used this same reasoning when rejecting affirmative action policies in education, as validation for his argument. Tschechtelin argues that society must move away from self-interest and, instead, deal honestly with the racial and ethnic problems that threaten the social, economic, and political stability of the nation.

In a telephone interview conducted in February 2001, Piedad Robertson, president of Santa Monica College in California, indicated that barriers to administrative and faculty positions are the same for all minorities.

Robertson cited the low numbers of minority students in doctoral programs and the fierce competition among community colleges, the private sector, and four-year institutions for those minority doctoral students. In addition, Robertson explained, the path to full-time faculty status involves a system that often does not reach out to minority candidates.

In a 2001 electronic interview, De los Santos, a Hispanic community college president, expressed a different perspective on the situation. According to De los Santos, in some parts of the country where the representation of African Americans is substantial, a candidate from another ethnic group might have difficulty being hired at an institution. On the other hand, it might be easier for a Hispanic to get a position in a community that is primarily Hispanic. In areas of the country where several ethnic groups are similarly represented, the hiring of minorities most likely depends on the screening committee and the person who makes the final decision. De los Santos stated that some college administrators work very hard to find ways to employ a more diverse faculty and staff, but that many administrators are weak in their resolve to recruit and employ minorities. Those administrators use legal decisions as an excuse not to do what needs to be done. It is a lot easier and, perhaps, politically safer if they do not go against current trends.

There are three other factors that should be included in any list of barriers to minority recruitment. These are: 1) the lack of readiness among faculty to reorganize around issues of cultural diversity, 2) an ingrained resistance to change, and 3) stereotypes held by some white faculty members that minority administrators are not psychologically and cognitively competent to perform high-level administrative tasks (Crase 1994).

Recruiting Minorities

Throughout the United States there are many efforts to get rid of affirmative action and to eliminate other programs that consider past discrimination. However, some educational leaders have recognized the dilemma and the need to hire members of historically under-represented groups. These leaders have initiated programs to help recruit and train individuals from minority groups.

Opp and Smith (1994) found eight strategies used by community colleges to recruit minorities:

1. Include minorities on boards of trustees.
2. Include minorities on search committees.
3. Include minorities on advisory boards.
4. Attend conferences concerned with minority issues.
5. Discuss job opportunities with minority business representatives.
6. Hire minorities as part-time adjunct faculty.
7. Discuss job opportunities with minority civic organizations.
8. Encourage faculty to contact minorities to publicize vacancies.

Even with the use of these strategies, the percentage of minority faculty employed by institutions is minimal.

The five-state survey found many of these strategies being used in the South. Another favorite strategy was advertising in publications designed to meet the career needs of minorities, such as *Black Issues in Higher Education*.

Respondents to the five-state survey were encouraged to identify other recruitment strategies that were not identified on the questionnaire. Five presidents indicated that they visited historically black colleges, and two indicated that they were "growing their own" by encouraging their graduates to prepare for community college teaching jobs and by publicizing successful minority graduates as role models.

It is clear that proactive strategies are needed if community colleges are to build a diverse faculty and administration. Without these strategies, the pool of minority applicants will remain small, and few minorities will be encouraged to seek employment at one of the nation's community colleges. Several ongoing initiatives are discussed below.

Schenectady County Community College

Schenectady County Community College, New York campus, created an intern program designed to increase faculty diversity. The program was started after the college affirmative action and multicultural affairs committee decided to address the lack of diversity among faculty members; out of more than 65 full-time faculty members, only three were minorities. Students also voiced the need for faculty diversity.

The program is designed to select an intern and give that person an overall knowledge of the entire community college operation. Minority candidates for the program usually are individuals with a master's degree and are pursuing a Ph.D. They intern for four semesters, teaching two courses per semester, assisting with advising and tutoring students, and attending faculty programs. After their training and teaching experience, these interns apply for vacancies as they become available.

San Diego and Imperial Counties Community College Association

The San Diego and Imperial Counties Community College Association (SDICCCA) is a consortium of nine community colleges in the San Diego area. The association worked with San Diego State University to create a community college training program, called "Internship," for members of underrepresented groups interested in community college teaching or counseling careers. The program identifies, recruits, trains, prepares, and helps place individuals from historically underrepresented groups as faculty and counselors in California community colleges. Each community college in the association accepts two to three interns per year.

In the recruitment phase, universities in the area and such organizations as the Urban League, the Asian Business Association, and the Chicano Federation are sent announcements and applications. Press releases are sent to minority and community newspapers. Each college participating in the consortium actively markets the program.

Students must apply for the program, and a committee screens applications. The committee selects 24 to 27 prospective interns, who then are invited in for a personal interview. Intern selections are made in late spring. Interns must have completed a master's degree or be in their last year of graduate school.

Interns are trained in the first year of the program, beginning in July. In July and August they attend a graduate institute at San Diego State University two evenings a week, where they learn about teaching and counseling in a community college. The institute awards three hours of graduate credit. During the fall semester, interns meet twice per month and discuss topics relevant to community colleges. Meetings rotate among the nine community colleges of the consortium. In the spring semester the interns meet once per month to discuss job search skills, résumé preparation, and interviewing skills. Throughout the year, each student works very closely with an assigned mentor. Interns observe classes, prepare materials for use in class, grade papers and tests, and teach selected class sessions.

After completing the program, interns are employed by one of the colleges as an adjunct instructor or counselor. During this phase of the training, the intern continues to work with his or her mentor and attends institute meetings one Friday per month to continue training.

The program has been very successful. During one three-year period, 70 interns participated in the program. Seventy percent were females, and 80% were minorities. A follow-up found that 75% of the participants were employed at a community college after completing the program.

Borough of Manhattan Community College

Recognizing that its student body is far more diverse than its faculty, the Borough of Manhattan Community College in New York developed a fellowship program aimed at recruiting minority teaching fellows. The college's student population is composed of approximately 43% blacks, 31% Hispanics, 10% Asians, and 9% whites, but the faculty is more than 66% white and only 25% black.

The minority fellowship program was started in the fall of 2000 and is designed to recruit teaching fellows from among minority graduates who hold a Ph.D. The fellows teach 12 hours per week under a mentor teacher and, after completing the program, they are given the opportunity to compete for an available faculty position at the community college. Through this initiative, the college seeks to enhance racial and ethnic diversity among faculty members.

City College of San Francisco

The City College of San Francisco (CCSF) has listed diversity as a key institutional value, and it is committed to employment practices that ensure diversity among faculty, staff, and administrators. To achieve this goal, CCSF established a Faculty/Mentor Diversity Internship. The purpose of this project is to assist CCSF in preparing people to become community college administrators, instructors, counselors, and librarians.

Interns learn and practice the teaching and interaction techniques appropriate for dealing with community college students, which will make the interns more competitive when applying for full- and part-time positions. To qualify, applicants must have a previous community college teaching experience (excluding teaching assistantships) and must have completed 50% of a master's degree program. An applicant also is eligible if he or she possesses an associate's degree and at least five years of full-time occupational experience or is within one year of obtaining an associate's degree with six or more years of full-time occupational experience and any required licenses or certificates.

CCSF also supports diversity by sponsoring the Annual World PULSE Diversity Retreat. The program is an interactive weekend of exploring cultural issues and identities, value differences, and the assumptions some may make about those unlike themselves. The retreat goes beyond just being culturally aware to enabling its participants to become more active in breaking down inequities around ethnicity, gender, age, sexual orientation, class, and physical or mental ability. Such an environment can only help the effort to recruit and retain a diverse faculty and administration.

CCSF may be more committed to diversity because of its history of electing culturally diverse presidents to its board of trustees. Lawrence Wong has served as past president of the board and is a recognized leader in promoting educational programs and services for immigrants, non-native speakers, minorities, and women and in efforts to diversify the college faculty and staff. Other past presidents include Rodel E. Rodis, who was the first Filipino American to be elected to public office in San Francisco, and Anita Grier, an African American with extensive experience in education administration. The current board president is Natalie Berg, a Jewish woman who has professional affiliations with the American Association of Women in Community and Junior Colleges, as well as the Association of Community College Administrators. Finally, Julio J. Ramos is a Puerto Rican board member committed to economic development and is dedicated to helping CCSF create programs that enable its diverse students to compete in the new economy.

Santa Monica Community College

Santa Monica Community College (SMCC) produces more minority transfer students for the University of California system and the California State system than any other community college in the state. Under the leadership of its president, SMCC not only talks about diversity but also has developed several programs to make it a reality.

At SMCC, the areas of greatest benefit are mentoring and "grow your own" activities. The college provides professional development, involving national organizations that promote underrepresented groups in higher education. SMCC works to encourage its minority faculty and staff, believing that continued exposure to new ideas causes people to grow. SMCC also supports its minority faculty by showcasing faculty publications. The college president and other key administrators and faculty also serve as active mentors to minority students.

In addition, SMCC has engaged in a new project with historically black colleges. A transfer agreement with a number of historically black institutions encourages African-American graduates to come to SMCC as professional employees, thus enriching the campus.

SMCC also works in underprivileged areas of Santa Monica to provide opportunities for young students. The college offers employment to teens to introduce them to the campus environment. Acceptance in that program is based on an individual's academic progress in high school. The best benefit of its strong mentoring program is the environment that is created by the effort — students and part-time faculty want to be a part of the family and end up seeking employment when vacancies occur.

University of Texas at Austin

The Community College Leadership Program at the University of Texas at Austin is part of an initiative to expand the pool of minority community college leaders. The program supports the education and development of community college leaders, giving special attention to minorities and those serving urban institutions.

Program activities are designed to assist promising community college mid-level managers and faculty of varied ethnic and cultural origins to achieve senior-level leadership positions in community colleges.

Miami-Dade Community College

The Teacher-Learning Project of Miami-Dade Community College is designed to change the institutional climate to accommodate the needs of nontraditional students, emphasizing diversity and learning styles. Mardee Jenrette, director of the Teaching-Learning Project, reports that the program has been successful and that the college has developed a faculty advancement program and a collegewide professional training center as the logical next step.

Santa Fe Community College

Santa Fe Community College near Gainesville, Florida, has made the commitment to enhance community relations and diversity as part of its institutional mission (Gillett-Karam, Roueche, and Roueche 1991). Santa Fe has created an Office of Ethnic Diversity. It also works in conjunction with the University of Florida to recruit and attract black doctoral students to the university while helping the community college develop its own black faculty members.

Conclusion

While many community college leaders talk about a desire to employ minorities, few have developed serious efforts to actively recruit or nurture minority employees. The institutions that have established initiatives to diversify their faculty and administrators should be applauded. Many more community colleges need to follow their lead and take action to make faculty and administrative diversity a priority.

Though there are factors that hinder community colleges from attracting minority faculty, that alone does not explain the paucity of minority faculty. Most institutions have done little to actively recruit them. It is not because qualified minority candidates do not exist. Many qualified minorities are searching actively for positions in community colleges but have been unable to find employment. And those who are hired as administrators often find themselves in lower-level staff positions in student services and multicultural or minority affairs positions, rather than more substantial leadership positions.

Because there are few academic programs designed to prepare community college instructors, community colleges historically have recruited high school teachers. This also limits diversity because teacher education programs report a shortage of minority students (AACC 1998). This shortage bodes ill for both public schools and community colleges and will require that community colleges greatly broaden their recruitment sources to include business and industry, the military, and other professions.

Based on the distribution of the population in the United States and assumptions about future immigrants, demographers predict that the American population will become more ethnically diverse in the first quarter of the 21st century (Solmon and Wingard 1991). Therefore it is imperative that community colleges adopt proactive strategies to hire more minorities. Some researchers assert that the struggle for minorities to acquire positions in higher education will be resolved by politics or judicial rulings. The institutions discussed above have initiated positive, proactive programs to hire minorities. One hopes that other community colleges will follow their lead.

References

Alger, J.R. "The Educational Value of Diversity." *Academe*. Washington, D.C.: American Association of University Professors, January-February 1997.

American Association of Community Colleges. *AACC Annual 1998-99 State-By-State Analysis of Community College Trends and Statistics*. Washington, D.C.: Community College Press, 1998.

Bowen, R.C., and Muller, G.H. *Achieving Administrative Diversity: New Directions for Community Colleges*. Washington, D.C.: Jossey-Bass, 1996. ERIC No. JC 960486.

Bramucci, R.L. "Community Colleges and the Workforce Investment Act: An Interview with Raymond L. Bramucci, Assistant Secretary of Labor for the Employment and Training Administration." *Community College Journal* 69 (July 1999): 41-44.

Crase, D. "The Minority Connection: African Americans in Administrative/Leadership Positions." *Physical Educator* 51, no. 1 (1994): 15-21.

Diversity Continuous Quality Improvement Team. "Strategic Conversation on Diversity: Maricopa Community College District." Final report presented to the Maricopa Community College District, October 1994. Available online at www.emc.maricopa.edu/diversity/diversity.html.

Evelyn, J. "Diversity Deferred in AACC Presidential Choice." *Black Issues in Higher Education* 17, no. 13 (2000): 24-27.

Fields, C.D. "Officials Look to Boost Minority Graduations at N.J. Colleges." *Black Issues in Higher Education* 17, no. 22 (2000): 16.

Foote, E. "Achieving Administrative Diversity." *New Directions for Community Colleges* 94, no. 1 (1996). ERIC No. ED395616.

Frengel, E. "Using Race-Based Scholarships." *Community College Journal* 69, no. 3 (1999): 18-22.

Gillett-Karam, R. "Midlevel Management in the Community College: A Rose Garden?" *New Directions for Community Colleges* 27 (Spring 1999): 5-11.

Gillett-Karam, R.; Roueche, S.D.; and Roueche, J.E. *Underrepresentation and the Question of Diversity: Women and Minorities in the Community College*. Washington, D.C.: Community College Press, 1991.

Hurd, H. "State Policies Greatly Impact Minority Access to Higher Education." *Black Issues in Higher Education* 17, no. 22 (2000): 18-19.

Kee, A.M. "Campus Climate: Perceptions, Policies and Programs in Community Colleges." *American Association of Community Colleges Research Brief*. AACC-RB-99-2. Washington, D.C.: Community College Press, 1999.

Kline, G. "Community College Faculty." *National Education Association Research Center Update* 1, no. 1 (2000): 1-4.

Opp, R.D., and Smith, A.B. "Minority Versus White Administrators' Perceptions of the Recruitment and Retention of Minority Faculty in Two-Year Colleges." *Journal of Applied Research in the Community College* 1 (Spring 1994): 85-99.

Phillippe, K.A., ed. *National Profile of Community Colleges: Trends and Statistics, 1997-1998*. Washington, D.C.: Community College Press, 1997.

Piercynski, M.; Matranga, M.; and Peltier, G. "Legislative Appropriation for Minority Teacher Recruitment: Did It Really Matter?" *Clearing House* 70, no. 4 (1997): 205-207.

Piland, W. E.; McFarlin, A.; and Murillo, L. "Intern." *Community College Journal* (1999): 31-37.

Solomon, L.C., and Wingard, T.L. "The Changing Demographics: Problems and Opportunities." In *The Racial Crisis in American Higher Education,* edited by P.G. Altbach and K. Lomotey. Albany: State University of New York Press, 1991.

Tschechtelin, J.D. "A White President of a Predominantly Black College Speaks Out About Race." *Community College Journal* 69, no. 3 (1999): 6-10.

Vaughan, G.B. "Paradox and Promise: Leadership and the Neglected Minorities." *New Directions for Community Colleges* 24 (Summer 1996): 5-12.

Wilds, D.J., and Wilson, R. *Minorities in Education 1997-98: Sixteenth Annual Status Report.* Washington, D.C.: American Council on Education, 1998.

Order Form

SHIP TO:		
STREET		
CITY/STATE OR PROVINCE/ZIP OR POSTAL CODE		
DAYTIME PHONE NUMBER		PDK MEMBER ROLL NUMBER

QUANTITY	*TITLE*	*PRICE*
	SUBTOTAL	
	Indiana residents add 5% Sales Tax	
	PROCESSING CHARGE	
	TOTAL	

ORDERS MUST INCLUDE PROCESSING CHARGE

Total Merchandise	*Processing Charge*
Up to $50	$5
$50.01 to $100	$10
More than $100	$10 plus 5% of total

Special shipping available upon request.
Prices subject to change without notice.

☐ Payment Enclosed (check payable to Phi Delta Kappa International)

Bill my ☐ VISA ☐ MasterCard ☐ American Express ☐ Discover

ACCT # DATE

EXP DATE / SIGNATURE

Mail or fax your order to: Phi Delta Kappa International,
P.O. Box 789, Bloomington, IN 47402-0789. USA
Fax: (812) 339-0018. Phone: (812) 339-1156

For fastest service, phone 1-800-766-1156 and use your credit card.